BRINESTAIN AND BISCUIT

Recipes and Rules
for Royal Navy Cooks

ADMIRALTY 1930

Introduction by
Edward Hampshire

the national archives

*The National Archives gratefully acknowledges
the generous help of Dr Margaret Billinghurst in the genesis
and development of this book.*

First published in 2006 by

The National Archives
Kew, Richmond
Surrey, TW9 4DU, UK

www.nationalarchives.gov.uk

The National Archives (TNA) was formed when
the Public Record Office (PRO) and Historical Manuscripts
Commission (HMC) combined in April 2003.

A catalogue card for this book is available from the British Library
ISBN 1 905615 09 4
978 1 905615 09 4

Jacket design, page design and typesetting by
Ken Wilson | Point 918

Printed in the UK by CPI Bath Press

CONTENTS

Introduction Cooking and Eating in the Royal Navy

B y general agreement, Britain has had a long and illustrious naval
history, the foundation of a once-mighty empire. In one respect,
though, there was little progression in over a hundred years.
At the end of the First World War, the food that the Royal Navy's
sailors ate, and the way it was prepared, cooked and served, had
changed little from the era of Nelson. The very first *Manual of Naval
Cookery*—highlights of which follow in these pages—was published in
1930, and it marks the beginning of a transition from a world of hammocks, mess-decks, 'cooks-of-the-day' and 'straight bakes' to the
bunk-beds, cafeteria eating, trained cooks and 'healthy eating' food
options of the 21st century.

   This gradual change, punctuated by dramatic developments
as a result of wartime necessity, foreign comparison and postwar
manning problems, is marked by the move from traditional cooking
and eating habits to 'general messing' (from the 1930s) and then
to modern 'centralized messing' (from the 1940s to the 1960s).

From Nelson to Jellicoe. Traditional messing arrangements—
standard in most British warships until after the Second World War
—placed the burdens of food preparation on individual members
of the mess (McKee, pp. 73–44; Baynham, pp. 109–14). Sailors slept,

ate and spent their free time largely on the same 'mess-deck': a large, open space populated by wooden benches and tables. Between 12 and 16 sailors, comprising one 'mess', would sit around each table, at which they would eat, play cards, read and drink their daily rum ration. At night, the benches, tables, cooking and eating implements would be cleared to the sides of the mess-deck, and hammocks slung from the ceiling. In theory, each sailor would have a space 18 inches (45 cm) wide within which to sling his hammock and get to sleep, and a total of 20 square feet (1.9 sq. m) allocated to him in the mess-deck; however, the reality could be closer to 16 square feet (1.5 sq. m) in some of the more cramped warships.

In this tight environment, food preparation was firmly under the control of each mess, with the galley's own cooks taking a clearly secondary role. Each mess-member would take it in turns to be the 'cook-of-the-day', in charge of preparing that day's catering. The role included receiving the daily food allocation; deciding what the meals would be and preparing them; taking the food to the galley for baking, cooking, frying or boiling; serving it up to one's messmates; and then clearing up afterwards. There was no formal training whatsoever for being a 'cook-of-the-day'. The new young sailor learned from his messmates, and the recipes—such as they were—were simply handed down from seaman to seaman.

The basic lunchtime dish—the bare minimum for a young sailor to learn, in order to survive the opprobrium of his messmates— was the 'straight bake'. This was a thick cut of meat, obtained from the ship's butcher, which would then be washed, basted and placed in a large dish (from the selection of pots and pans kept by each mess); potatoes would be peeled, cut and placed with onions around the meat, and the dish then passed to the galley cooks for roasting. Other basic meals included toad-in-the-hole and 'pot-mess', essentially a stew with meat, dumplings, carrots, potatoes and any other vegetables that were available.

Additional food items could be purchased to add to the basic provision for each mess. This was where the more ambitious cooks-of-the-day would come into their own: for example, using the daily mess supplement to buy dough, which he would roll out on the mess table and add raisins to make a pie, or to buy additional vegetables such as turnips, onions, cabbage and peas. Green vegetables would often be boiled in a muslin bag alongside any meat and potatoes. Tinned and possibly fresh fruit might also be purchased, as might flour for baking or tea for each mess. Such additions to the basic requirement were supplied by the ship's 'canteen', while the basic allocation of food was handed out direct from the paymaster's stores.

Modernization and wartime. The system of food preparation described above, instantly recognizable to any sailor from the Napoleonic era to the Great War, could have considerable disadvantages for the sailor, particularly if his mess had more than its fair share of poor cooks. It did, though, have the advantage of encouraging sailors to learn extremely quickly to become at least competent in some of the mess basics: responsibility for sailors' food and nutrition in the end rested with the consumers themselves, and a hungry mess was an unhappy mess. At its core was the naval ethos of companionship and trust. You did not just live in close proximity to, work with and fight alongside your messmates; you also sustained them through the four main meals of the day: breakfast, lunch, tea and supper.

After the First World War, however, it was becoming clear that the disadvantages of the system were outweighing the advantages. Untrained cooks too often meant indifferently or badly made meals and the wasting of stores. The average Tar's rudimentary (or non-existent) appreciation of the importance of a balanced diet meant that sailors could easily lack the nutrition they needed. Despite a number of improvements in the quality and variety of daily allocations of food to messes in the early 20th century, the old, essentially 18th-century mode of preparation was manifestly outdated—and perhaps even dangerous for a modern warship's fighting efficiency.

From the late 1920s steps were gradually taken to improve the situation. The move to 'general messing' was tentatively begun, whereby food preparation was done by the galley cooks in enlarged galleys, and the cook-of-the-day role shrank to that of bringing the cooked food from the galley to his messmates. The first parts of the Navy to move to general messing appear to have been the training establishments and shore barracks. In the former, the lack of time available to prepare food and almost complete absence of experienced sailors to help meant a diet that one seaman complained consisted of potatoes and little else (according to Baynham, p. 112). Another step was the creation of ship's canteen committees—led by an officer and made up of mess-deck representatives—to help regulate and improve the quality of the

additional stores purchased from the canteen. The taking-over
of the running of each ship's canteen by the Navy, Army and Air
Force Institution (the NAAFI) also helped improve the situation.

A further stage was the writing of the *Manual* reproduced in
this book. Alongside two other slightly later manuals focusing
on traditional messing, this was the Royal Navy's first systematic
attempt to lay down standards for general-mess cooking and to
instil a modicum of nutritional understanding in its cooks and
sailors. It is within this context that the 'principles of cooking'
and the listing of possible meat 'diseases' in the *Manual* should
be understood. In the third chapter, the sheer quantity of food
necessary for feeding a ship's crew is brought home. At this time,
the largest vessels in the Navy—the battleships, battle-cruisers and
aircraft carriers—would have had crews of 1000 or more, a typical
cruiser would have had 500, and a destroyer, the workhorse of
the fleet, between 150 and 200 men. However, even the quantities
invoked in the *Manual* pale besides those needed for a whole fleet
of battleships, carriers, cruisers and destroyers. Preparations in
the 1930s for supplying the fleet in event of a war in the Far East
produced the following staggering figures for feeding 60,000 sailors
for only 15 days: 660,000 lbs (300 tonnes) of flour; 500,000 lbs (227
tonnes) of frozen beef; 120,000 lbs (54.5 tonnes) of margarine;
240,000 lbs (109 tonnes) of sugar; 39,000 lbs (almost 18 tonnes) of
tea; 9000 gallons (40,915 litres) of naval rum; and 40,000 lbs (just
over 18 tonnes) of cigarettes (National Archives, ADM 1/4050).

Despite the new emphasis on nutrition and good cooking by
the Admiralty, there were still many flaws in the approach. These

would be worryingly exposed during the Second World War. One problem was that during the interwar period general messing was introduced only in the very largest vessels, and its adoption on cruisers was slow and piecemeal. Furthermore, general messing also met with some resistance from sailors used to preparing their own food—protests on the new cruiser HMS *Penelope* reaching as far as the Admiralty Secretariat in 1937 (National Archives, ADM 12/1735, code 103.3).

Another flaw was the quality of general-messing food preparation: the main concern of the sailors themselves. A complaint from Chatham barracks, in Kent, exposed the problem (National Archives, ADM 1/19118). In this instance, the introduction of general messing had not resulted in any increase in the size of the galley, despite the transfer of food preparation responsibilities. In a time of financial constraints and high unemployment, an opportunity was thus taken to cut costs at the expense of the quality of food. In addition there remained no centralized school of naval cookery, and many of the galley cooks were no more than the 'boil-it-or-bake-it' merchants of the traditional-messing variety.

A further problem was the quality of the food and ingredients themselves. In home waters, vessels were allocated Ministry of Food bulk supplies, which, often having been in storage for some time, could leave much to be desired. At the end of the Second World War a survey of sailors' least favourite foods put Ministry of Food '3rd grade salmon' at the top, with such unappetizing examples as tinned bacon (prone to 'splintering' into many pieces when boiled), tinned steak and kidney pudding (known by sailors as 'babies' heads', and still served today) and corned beef ('corned dog') not far behind (National Archives, ADM 1/21707).

A final problem, involving the habitability of vessels in general, was the ever-reducing space in ships for messing. As the war progressed, additional equipment such as radar and new weapons was added at the expense of sailors' living space. Emergency wartime vessels, such as the famous Flower-class corvettes, had atrocious living and eating conditions. In these ships, the sailors' accommodation was high in the bows and thus subject to much vomit-inducing vertical and lateral motion, while the galley was located near the stern, meaning it was accessible only from the outside. This left the sailors open to the elements when collecting food to take to the mess-decks (see Brown, pp. 102–3, 134–55 and 189).

The era of floating cafeterias. A comparison with US-built war-ships, many of which were transferred to the Royal Navy during the war via the 'lend-lease' arrangement, is revealing. The American ships had such luxuries as machine laundries, mechanical potato peelers and even ice-cream makers and soda fountains. Above all, they had cafeteria service—a separate dining hall set aside for eating, rather than the Royal Navy's practice of combining living, eating and sleeping in one increasingly cramped room (see Brown, pp. 134–5). The Navy had considered introducing cafeteria service and bunk-beds just before the war, for HMS *Belfast* and her sister ship HMS *Edinburgh* (National Archives, ADM 12/1735, Code 103.3); but this plan had been overtaken by hostilities, and it was not until the completion of the Navy's last battleship, HMS *Vanguard*, in 1946 that these improvements began to be implemented.

An initial lack of seating space in the mess-decks, which were now crammed with bunk-beds, might well be what lay behind a 'near mutiny' on the *Vanguard* (see Brown and Moore, pp. 182–4). However, given the nature of discussions on the new carrier HMS *Eagle* a few years later, the problem might well have been the strange *form* of cafeteria service introduced in *Vanguard*, where sailors had food brought to them on large trays. This type of service, with its residual element of the old cook-of-the-day arrangements, was extremely costly in manpower and resulted in considerable delays serving food, as it was difficult to find enough spare sailors to act as waiters. It was quickly replaced by the standard self-service arrangements that were introduced in the larger postwar ships (National Archives, ADM 1/21711).

As postwar austerity turned into the full-employment consumer society of the late 1950s and 1960s, the Navy began to enter a manning crisis that made efforts to improve life at sea a priority. In the new destroyers and frigates that now formed the backbone of the fleet, general messing and bunks were introduced, although a system whereby sailors sat on the bottom of three bunks to eat their meals proved deeply unpopular (not least with those unfortunate enough to have been allocated the bottom bunk!). By the 1970s a true cafeteria system had developed, with separate dining rooms, and sleeping areas with both bunks and seating. And by 1970 the area allocated for junior ratings in new ships had increased to 25 square feet (2.3 sq. m), 4 square foot (0.4 sq. m) of which was given to providing dining-hall space. In addition, the range of food available at the cafeteria and the NAAFI (including what sailors call 'nutty'—sweets and chocolate) at last began to approach that in US vessels.

Finally, in a significant break with naval tradition, the centuries-old rum issue was replaced in 1971 by an allocation of two cans of beer a day per sailor. This was one category where sailors would have agreed that the Royal Navy had the upper hand over the US Navy, whose warships were (and are) completely free of alcohol! (See Brown and Moore, pp. 182–4).

This brings us to the present day. In the Navy's most recent class of destroyers, the Type 45, the old mess has almost disap-peared altogether: junior ratings will be accommodated in spacious six-berth cabins, have access to large recreation spaces, gyms and cafeterias, and have a total space allocation probably approaching three times that of sixty years ago—a far cry from the cramped conditions on the Dreadnoughts of the First World War. In 75 years or so, the Royal Navy has come a long way in terms of sustaining and feeding its men (and now women). The 1930 *Manual* reproduced here was to become one of the first and most important steps in transforming living standards for the ordinary British sailor.

Edward Hampshire
Modern Records Specialist, The National Archives

CHAPTER I

GENERAL INSTRUCTIONS

Cleanliness

It is strongly impressed on all connected with the handling, preparation and cooking of food that scrupulous cleanliness is imperative in the person and in the preparing room and galley and with all implements.

The Senior Cook Rating in each galley is held responsible for the cleanliness of the galley, plant and implements and of all persons employed therein.

CLEANING GEAR REQUIRED

Hot water, soda, soap, salt, scrubbers and clean cloths (not flannel or woollen material).

TO CLEAN WOODWORK

Hard soap and water only must be used. On no account use soda or soft soap as these discolour the wood. After being scrubbed with soap and water, wood work should be well rinsed with a good supply of clean water.

TO CLEAN UTENSILS

All utensils after use should at once be filled with hot soda water, with the exception of articles which are made of aluminium, as follows:—

Iron Saucepans, etc. —Hot soda water and yellow soap. When clean, rinse with hot water and dry with a clean cloth.

Tin and Enamelled Vessels.—Clean as above and polish tinware outside with whitening mixed to a paste with cold water. Great care must be taken to wipe the whitening from corners. Stains in enamel can be removed by rubbing with salt.

Copper Utensils.—Great care must be taken in cleaning these vessels, rub well with salt, wash off with hot soda water until all stains are removed.

Aluminium.—Soda should not be used in cleaning vessels made of aluminium as galvanic action is set up when in contact with another metal. Vinegar, for the same reason, should not be kept in aluminium vessels.

TO CLEAN OVENS

Galley ovens must be frequently cleaned. This can be done by using hot water applied with a mop or long-handled broom.

STEAM COOKERS AND BOILING COPPERS

Scrub out after use with water, soda and hard soap, and rub dry with a cloth. The trays of steam cookers should be removed and cleaned separately. On no account should corrosives, such as caustic soda or cleaning powders, be used.

NOTE.—Sand should never be used to clean utensils as

there is always the risk of particles of sand remaining and being mixed with the food.

Organisation of Galley Staff

It is the duty of the C.P.O. Cook or Senior Cook Rating in charge of a galley to organise and supervise the Cooks' Staff. Whilst no hard and fast rule can be laid down, suitable to every class of ship, in general the system of three watches is recommended:—

> 1st watch on duty from 1200 until 1200 next day (to be arranged as follows:—watch take on duty from 1200 until supper is served and galleys cleaned up, the watch turning out the next morning according to the requirements of the menu).
>
> 2nd watch (Stand-by-Watch) on duty from 0730 until 1600 or later if required.
>
> 3rd watch who go off duty at 1200 until 0730 the next morning.

And so on in rotation.

> This ensures:—
>
> 3 watches working together during the Forenoon.
>
> 2 watches during the afternoon, Stand-by-Watch working later if required.
>
> 1 watch working during the Dog and Morning Watches.

When in Home Ports this system can be extended into a Four Watch System. He should furthermore organise his staff so that each rating has as far as possible some definite duty to perform for which he will be held responsible. This is best achieved by dividing the staff into sub-sections, the Senior Cook Rating supervising the whole.

EXAMPLE DURING THE FORENOON

Soup. Making and Distribution	1 Rating.
Roast Meats and Oven work in general	2 Ratings.
Vegetables. Cooking and Distribution	2 Ratings.
Sweet. Cooking and Distribution	2 Ratings.
Preparing and General Cleaning	Remainder.

Organisation will enable the staff to keep the galley clean with the minimum loss of time. Each rating should be given some definite section of the galley to keep clean, and for which he will be held responsible in addition to his cooking duties, *e.g.* the cook ratings working the oven should be held responsible that the cooking range is externally and internally clean.

Duties of Senior Cook Rating in connection with General Messing

Where the victualling is carried out on the General Mess system, the satisfaction and comfort of the ship's company depend to a great degree upon the constant variation of the menu, and upon the skill and attention given by the cooks to every detail connected with the preparation, cooking, carving and serving up of the food.

The Senior Cook Rating is to assist the officer in charge of the General Mess with any suggestions which occur to him for the variation of the menu, new dishes or any other improvement in the messing of the ship's company, and is to give constant attention to the work of the cooks at all stages in the preparation and serving of the meals.

He is responsible that the lower ratings are instructed on all matters in connection with their duties, including the correct carving of meats and the proper serving of the dishes, as well as the preparation and cooking of meals, and is expected to continue afloat the training which has been commenced in the schools on shore.

On receipt of all articles of food supplied to the galley, he is to check the weights with those shown on the galley distribution list, and should any differences be found, he is to report such to the General Mess Office.

In addition, he is carefully to examine the quantities of the ingredients supplied for each dish, and if in his opinion the quantities are either insufficient or in excess of requirements, he is to report the fact to the General Mess Office, in order that the point may be referred to the Accountant Officer.

After satisfying himself that the weights and quantities are correct, he will, where lockers are provided, lock up such stores as are not required for immediate use and he will be held responsible that no misappropriation takes place.

Any defect in the quality of the raw material supplied to him, even though it is fit for issue, should be brought to the notice of the General Mess Office.

When meat is supplied to the galley, the Senior Cook Rating is to take care that the proper joints and pieces are selected for roasting, pies, puddings, hashes and stews, and that in cutting up, all remains of meat, fat and bone are put on one side in clean receptacles, lean meat and bones for the stock-pot, and the fat for clarifying.

He is also responsible that the following instructions are complied with:—

1. No dishes are to be cooked earlier than is absolutely necessary, and none are ever to be cooked or part cooked overnight without the express permission of the Accountant Officer.

2. When carving takes place prior to the issue to the ship's company, it is to be done as late as possible before each meal, and when carved, the meat is to be placed in dishes in the hot lockers with the least possible delay.

3. The food is to be properly and evenly distributed among the messes in accordance with the numbers victualled in each, all distribution is to take place by weight and measure and never by eye, and the scale laid down herein, or as amended by the Accountant Officer, is to be strictly adhered to.

4. Private meals are not to be cooked in the galley, and no one other than the Cooks' Staff is to be allowed in the galley, bakery or serving lobbies.

5. No meals are to be served from the galley until "Cooks"

is sounded, except as may be specially arranged for watch keepers.

6. A list of the issue of meat dishes to the messes is to be kept, and a cook rating is to be detailed when "clear up decks" is sounded to muster them on their return, any shortage being reported.

7. In the event of any mess with a complaint bringing back either a meal or any portion of it to the galley, the Senior Cook Rating is responsible that the matter is immediately brought to the notice of the Accountant Officer for investigation. Complaints should not be received unless presented by the Caterer of the Mess.

8. Galleys, bakeries, kitchens, or preparing rooms are not to be used as messes or wash places; no smoking is to take place therein, nor are wet clothes to be dried in them.

9. Keys are to be returned to the Keyboard by the Senior Cook Rating on board and drawn by the Senior Hand turning out.

PRECAUTIONS AGAINST FIRE

The Senior Cook Rating is to take care that a sufficient supply of sand is kept in a readily accessible position in the galley for extinguishing a fire. Water is never to be used for this purpose. In the event of fire occurring in the galley, all ventilation including doors, scuttles, hatches, supply and exhaust fans are to be immediately closed and the outbreak reported to the O.O.W. The controllers of fans should be in readily accessible positions which should be known to the galley staff.

The galley staff is to be fully acquainted with the orders for the prevention of fire.

> In oil-fired galleys the main stop valve to oil supply is to be closed and the motor switched off.
>
> Drip-tins and save-alls are to be kept dry, and any oil spilled on the deck should be wiped up at once.
>
> Fryers are not to contain oil or fat above one-third capacity.
>
> Fat is never to be rendered down in open tins either in any oven or on top of the hot-plates, but is to be put in pots with water and clarified by boiling.

Machinery and Plant

Special attention is drawn to the danger of inserting the hand in any power-driven appliances, particularly slicing and pul-verising machines, dough mixers and kneaders. Only ratings who have been fully instructed are to be allowed to work machines, and the work is invariably to be closely super-intended by a Chief or Petty Officer. In the Hobart, and sim-ilar machines, the hand is on no account to be inserted and the rammer is to be invariably used. Any rating seen to insert his hand is to be reported to the Accountant Officer. Attention is called to the Admiralty Order directing that when instructions are disregarded Hurt Certificates will not be granted in case of accidents.

POTATO PEELING MACHINES

Care should be taken that the machine is not overloaded. The running ports should be kept well lubricated, defects reported and the electrical gear frequently inspected by the proper ratings. The potatoes should be tipped out of the sack and freed from superfluous dirt and stones, before being placed in the peeler.

A plentiful supply of water must be used when peeling potatoes, and after peeling, the potatoes must be well washed and placed in clean cold water.

SLICING MACHINES

Hand and Power Driven.—The efficient working of any slicing machine depends entirely upon the movable parts. These should be kept thoroughly clean and well lubricated. The knife must be sharpened before and after use. The rating working the machine should always stand on cocoanut matting (battened to the deck) if the deck gets wet or slippery. The knife should be completely covered with a guard when not in use. The electrical gear should be inspected by duly qualified ratings at least once a week.

THE HOBART MINCING MACHINE

Special attention is drawn to the danger of inserting the hand in the machine whilst in motion; the wooden rammer is always to be used. After use the machine, when completely stopped, must be taken to pieces, the various parts being washed in hot soda water and thoroughly dried to prevent rust. The knives should be frequently sharpened on the lap plate provided, and care should be taken that fragments of bone are not put into the machine. The fibre washers should be renewed frequently in order to avoid undue wear of the worm, cutters or knives. The running parts of the machine should be kept well oiled and the electrical gear should be inspected by duly qualified ratings at least once a week.

Should the machine become choked, no attempt is to be made to clear it while the knives are in motion. The machine is to be completely stopped, the break collar, cutting knife and spindle removed, cleaned and replaced.

It is recommended that the switch controlling the Hobart Machine be placed in a position easily within reach of the operator.

POTATO CHIPPING MACHINE

Care is to be taken in the use of these machines. Potatoes are to be passed through the cutter with one smooth continuous pull on the handle. Any irregular forcing or sudden jerking will almost certainly result in snapping the cast iron handle of the machine. Scrupulous cleanliness is essential with these machines, particular attention being paid to the cutter.

DOUGH MIXING AND KNEADING MACHINES

The Senior Cook Rating in charge of the bakery should acquaint himself with the instructions relating to bakeries and bakery plant, and should especially impress upon the junior ratings the danger of tampering with the safety locking device fitted to these machines, and of attempting to handle the dough while the knives are in motion. Hurt Certificates will not be granted in case of accidents due to neglect or disobedience of this order, and a notice to this effect is to be prominently displayed in all bakeries.

When the slippery condition of the deck in the bakery renders it advisable, steps are to be taken to fit cocoanut matting for battening down on the deck.

STEAM CHESTS

Severe scalding may result from opening a steam chest without taking the necessary precaution of first shutting off the steam and draining the chest. A notice embodying detailed instructions regarding the precautions to be taken prior to the opening of steam chests, and including a warning of possible danger if the steam pressure is excessive, is to be posted in a conspicuous position in the galley.

Principles of Cooking

Food is cooked for the following reasons:—

(a) To render meat and vegetables more digestible by loosening the muscular fibres in meats and by breaking up the starch grains in vegetables.

(b) To make it more appetising to sight, to smell and to taste, and for this reason it is essential that every endeavour should be made to ensure that dishes are as attractive in appearance as possible, and that made-up dishes should be actually tasted in the course of preparation.

(c) To ensure the destruction of bacteria and parasites.

Roasting and Baking.—Whilst proper roasting consists of cooking meat by suspension in the direct heat of an open fire, it is a method which is now rarely practised; equally satisfactory results can more conventionally be obtained in a properly ventilated oven. Roasting is the most popular method of cooking although one of the most expensive.

Boiling.—This is one of the simplest ways of cooking. It implies immersing the food to be cooked in boiling liquid, not necessarily water, for a certain length of time.

The following foods must be kept actually boiling all the time of cooking:—

(a) All green vegetables and most other kinds of vegetables.
(b) All bone and meat soups.
(c) All boiled puddings.
(d) Starch grains in the forms of rice, macaroni, flour (in sauces), etc.

Steaming.—Steaming is usually performed by steam passing from a close boiler to a close chamber or by placing a steamer over a boiler containing water. It is the slowest of all methods of cookery.

Grilling and Broiling.—Both of these methods imply cooking meat, fish, etc., over or before a clear fire. It is rather an extravagant way of cooking, as only the best cuts of meat, etc., can be successfully treated by this means. It is a quick method of cooking, and if properly done, the results are digestible and savoury.

Frying.—This, the quickest of all cooking methods, is cooking food in smoking hot fat or oil. Cheap pieces of meat with tough fibres should never be fried, the quick cooking only rendering them more tough and hard. As it is both bad for digestion and unpleasant in appearance to have grease adhering to fried foods, they should be lifted out of the fat on to a piece of clean paper.

Stewing.—This is the most economical and nourishing of all methods, as the liquid is invariably served as gravy or syrup, and so whatever good is extracted from the meat, fruits, etc., is partaken of in the liquid. A stew should never be allowed to bubble or boil; gentle simmering is the best and only way of obtaining a tender and good-looking stew. "Cook long and cook slowly" is a golden counsel for the attainment of ideal stews.

Meats—Descriptions of, and Their Diseases

Meat may be supplied in one of three conditions: Fresh Killed, Chilled or Frozen.

Fresh Beef.—The fat is of a creamy white or even yellow colour and the flesh a deep, rich crimson. It is dry to the touch and no moisture can be squeezed out.

Chilled Beef.—The fat is of a lighter colour, flushed with a pale pink and the flesh of a light red, and the surface does not dry.

Frozen Beef.—The fat is a dead, waxy white, the flesh is a darker shade of red than in fresh killed, and on defrosting often assumes a very dark colour. The freezing process robs the meat of none of its nutritive qualities, and bad cooking alone can make frozen meat appear at a disadvantage with freshly killed meat.

Frozen Mutton.—Is principally imported from New Zealand, and is of the best quality, equal to our English Southdown Mutton.

Pork.—As supplied, is always freshly killed. The colour of the flesh should be brownish pink and of fine texture with an abundance of fat between the muscles, the fat should be white and the rind thin. In old animals, the flesh is dark red, less fat, and the flesh on being cooked gives off an odour of urine.

Veal.—The flesh should be pale pink and should not be flabby, tear easily or have the appearance of being water-soaked. The fat should be plentiful and very white, especially that surrounding the kidney.

Veal and Pork.—Are rich in gelatine, the best possible medium for the propagation of bacteria of all descriptions. It follows that both should be well and thoroughly cooked; if imperfectly cooked, the consequences to the consumer may be very serious.

Bacon.—The fat of hams and bacon should be firm and

white, the flesh firm and free from holes. Any tinge of colour in the fat is suspicious. Bacon can be tested for sweetness by probing the thick portions of the meat with a skewer.

Tripe.—The stomach of an ox requires the greatest care in cleansing to render it fit for consumption. For this reason, it is recommended that tripe should not be used in the summer months.

Freezing Meat.—The meat usually supplied to the Service is frozen beef and mutton. Beef has, as a rule, been frozen hard in a temperature of from 10 degrees to 15 degrees Fahrenheit as soon as the animal heat has left the carcase.

Defrosting.—Whenever possible, the quarters or sides should be defrosted without cutting, so as to avoid draining the meat of its chief nutriment, the residue of the blood, which drains away through each cut with the fluid thrown off in thawing.

The cook should take care that no damaged or deteriorated meat is used. Such meat may be detected:—

By its discoloration; the fat of beef will be very pale and the lean dark brown or black, the mutton will be misshapen.

By rubbing the palm of a warm hand on the fat of either beef or mutton for a few seconds; if the meat is stale there will be a distinct, tallowy smell.

If bruises are noticed in any quarters of beef, they should be cut to see if the bruises extend internally.

Diseased Meat.—The cook should as far as possible endeavour that no meat which is diseased is used in the preparation of any dish. A superficial examination of the sides, quarters or carcases will fail to disclose many diseases to which they are liable, and it is only on cutting up that their presence may be detected.

The chief indication of the presence in the meat of any real disease is to be found in the glands, of which there are a number throughout the carcase, and which will be met with in the process of cutting up. When the carcase is that of a healthy animal, the glands will be of a brownish pink colour and gelatinous in appearance.

The diseases, etc., which the cook may be expected to detect are:—

Tuberculosis.—The glands are enlarged and full of a dark grey, gritty substance; in addition, nodules of a similar substance may be found on the inside of the ribs or underneath the diaphragm. Portions of the lungs may be found adhered to the inside of the ribs. Special attention should be paid to pork, which is particularly liable to this disease.

Hydatids, Cysts.—Commonly known as tapeworms. Meat so infected is frequently termed measly beef or pork. The indications are a small mass of jelly-like substance found in the muscles of the pig. In the jelly is a small white cyst within which is the tapeworm. The usual place of infection in pork is the shoulder, the neighbourhood of the brisket and diaphragm.

MUTTON
Mode of cutting up

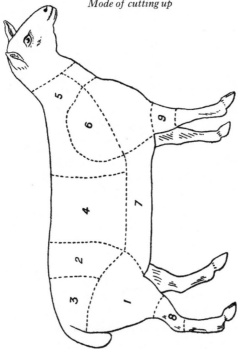

1. The Leg.	5. The Neck.
2. The Loin. Thick End.	6. The Shoulder.
3. The Loin. Chump End.	7. The Breast.
4. The Saddle.	8 & 9. The Shanks.

Roastings . . . . Nos. 1, 2, 3, 4, 6.
Stewings . . . . 5, 7.
Broths & Soup . . . . . 8 & 9.
Boilings . . . . . No. 1.

MODE OF CUTTING UP MEAT
BULLOCK

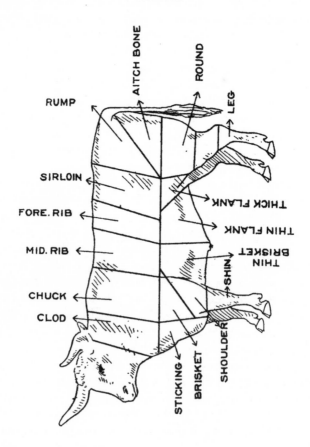

In beef it is more uncommon. The cyst is much larger, and not so dangerous a parasite as that found in pork. Tapeworms may also be found in mutton and in rabbit.

Flukes.—A small, flat worm about an inch long and shaped like a sole found in the liver of sheep. In cutting up the liver, it will be found lodged in the pipes.

Bone Taint.—Difficult to detect before the meat is cut up. It is caused by putrefaction setting in, in the deeper parts of the carcase, whilst the outside remains frozen, and is due to the carcase being placed in the freezing chamber before the animal heat has been entirely eliminated. It will be immediately detected in the process of disjointing, and if suspected may be tested for by inserting a skewer into the deeper parts of the meat close to the bone. The whole carcase or quarter is not necessarily affected.

Brine Stain.—Caused by the drips from leaky pipes and joints in the refrigerating chamber. A carcase so infected has on the outside a dirty greenish-brown stain; the contaminated surface may be cut away and disclose an apparently clean and healthy sub-surface, but on placing in heat, such as for cooking, the meat gives off an unpleasant and pungent odour rendering it entirely unfit for food.

Brine stain does not necessarily affect the whole of the carcase or quarter in which it occurs. The affected parts can generally be cut away and the remainder of the meat utilised.

Fly-blown.—In hot weather, meat may become "fly-blown." This is most common in the thinner portions and in parts which are blood-stained. Fly-blown meat has a very strong smell, but the portions affected may generally be cut off and the remainder used, if sweet.

Fish, Description of

There are three classes of fish:—

(1) Oily fish, such as salmon, eels, herrings and mackerel. The flesh of these fish is dark, because the oil is distributed throughout the flakes, and, although it is richer and more nutritious than the flesh of white fish, it is more difficult to digest.

(2) White fish, such as whiting, soles, cod and plaice. The oil, or fat, in these fish is stored in the liver, with the result that the flesh is light, digestible, and particularly white in appearance. For invalids, white fish should always be selected, never the oily kinds.

(3) Shell fish, such as oysters, crabs, lobsters, etc. These fish, with the exception of the almost self-digesting oyster, are less wholesome than other classes, owing to the close texture of the flesh.

All varieties of fish do not keep equally well. Halibut, cod, haddock, plaice and flat fish may be kept on ice for a week, but whiting, mackerel and herrings should be used at once. The cod and flat fish improve with keeping for a day or two.

Apart from staleness and decomposition certain diseases attack fish, but cooking renders their condition harmless.

When permission has been given by the Accountant

Officer for fish caught alongside to be cooked in the galley, should it be uncertain whether such fish is poisonous or not, a small piece of silver should be boiled with it; if it be poisonous, the silver will turn black.

The greatest care should be exercised in this matter, especially on foreign stations, since the fish caught in sluggish, shallow and warm water are not only rarely palatable but frequently dangerous to the consumer.

On no account should shell fish brought by any member of the ship's company be cooked in the galley without the express permission of the Accountant Officer.

The fish commonly used are:—

Cod.—Best season October to February. Head should be large, tail small, shoulders thick; liver creamy white, and the skin clear silvery with a bronze-like sheen.

Whiting.—Best in December, January and February. Should be of a bright silvery appearance, have no barbell, nor show the "thumb-marks" seen on haddock. The flesh deteriorates very quickly and must be eaten when fresh.

Haddock.—Best between November and February. Should be bronze coloured and white belly. Has the "Apostle's or Thumb Mark" on the shoulder and a barbell. Young haddocks are sometimes supplied as whiting.

Hake.—Best from June to January. Has a long body and rough scales and no barbell. A characteristic of hake is that although perfectly fresh its flesh is readily detached from the bones.

Plaice.—In season all the year round. The body should be thick with orange spots on the dark upper surface; the white side should have a pinkish, not bluish, tint.

Sole.—In season all the year round. Upper side dark brown without coloured spots, underside creamy white. Keeps very badly.

Brill.—In season all the year round. A flat fish, the eyes of which are on the left side. The skin on the upper side should be unwrinkled and with smooth scales, the underside a creamy white.

Herrings.—Seasons vary and the fish are available nearly all the year round. Herrings must be fresh. The fish are caught in drift nets and for this reason are subject to damage and laceration. Such fish are known in the trade as "TB's" (torn bellies), and have no market value since deterioration is rapid. It is not allowable to pack them in salt. Care should be taken that such damaged fish are not supplied to H.M. Ships.

Mackerel.—Best in August, September and October. The marking on the skin should be very bright and distinct, and the underside creamy white. Its keeping qualities are very poor.

Pilchards.—Like herrings but much smaller, are fatter and have larger scales. Unlike herrings the under jaw is turned up.

Lobsters, Shrimps and Prawns.—The tails, when pulled out straight and then loosened, should spring back and clip tightly against the body. Lobsters with incrustations on the shell are usually old and tough.

Dietary, Food Values

Food is necessary to provide material for the growth and repair of the living body tissues, and to supply energy which can be converted into heat and work.

The body is composed of a number of elements, the chief of which are:—Oxygen, Hydrogen, Nitrogen, Carbon, Calcium, Phosphorus, Sulphur, and Iron. These elements are contained in the foods we eat. During the process of digestion, the complex components of food are broken up into simpler ones which can be taken up by the body fluids, and utilised to fulfil the two great functions of food.

The essential constituents of a dietary (*sic*) are: —

Water.
Proteins.
Fats.
Carbohydrates.
Inorganic salts.
Vitamins.

Experiments on animals have shown that death ensues when any one of these six units is withdrawn from the diet for a sufficient length of time.

Serving of Meals

It is of great importance that food should be presented in as attractive a manner as possible. Whilst good cooking makes an appeal to the senses of taste and smell, the manner in which food is served appeals to the eye. The success of a meal depends almost as much upon good appearance as upon cooking and seasoning. Good food is improved by good serving whilst a little care and forethought will make an excellent meal from the most unpromising materials.

Foods which should be served hot must be really hot and not insipidly warm. Foods which should be served cold should be cold and not partially warm.

The method of arranging food in dishes, the colourings employed and the garnishes used should be varied; monotony in food is fatal, the eye of the consumer fails after a time to be pleased with a garnish that is served up with unfailing regularity.

Meals served in ordinary service mess traps can be attractive and appetising in appearance. To achieve this result, attention should be paid to the following points:—

(1) Cleanliness and neatness.
(2) Arrangement with a sense of balance.
(3) Garnishing.
(3) Colour.

CLEANLINESS AND NEATNESS

The dishes should be clean internally and externally, there should not be any part of the food showing in the margin of the dish; this white space has an important effect of creating a sense of sweetness. The food should always be neatly arranged in order.

ARRANGEMENT WITH BALANCE

The food should be placed in the dish with a sense of balance; if an imaginary line is drawn across the centre of the dish, then the food equally divided, the necessary balance will be secured. Food so arranged is generally pleasing to the eye of the consumer.

GARNISHING

The attractiveness of a dish depends to a great extent upon the use of garnishes. The object of all garnishes is to improve the appearance of the dish, so that it will have a pleasing exterior. When the garnish has to be cooked, it is advisable to cook it separately, ornamenting the dish just before serving.

The following garnishes can be used with advantage when serving:—

Soups.—Carrots and turnips, cut into shapes such as:—circles and squares, five, six and eight pointed stars. Full, half and quarter moons with crinkled edges. Vermicelli broken into small pieces, cucumber thinly sliced.

Fish.—Leaves of parsley, chopped and powdered parsley, fried parsley, hard boiled eggs, lemons, cucumbers and beetroots thinly sliced.

Meat.—Watercress, vermicelli, shaped vegetables, breadcrumbs, parsley.

Sweets.—Angelica, *glacé* fruits cut into various shapes, coloured cocoanut, pistachio kernels.

COLOUR

Colours have the effect of attracting or repelling the eye. To attract and please, colour should harmonise or blend. The following two rules will be a guide with foods:—

(1) Relieve dark backgrounds with light colours.
(2) Relieve light backgrounds with delicately-tinted colours.

For instance, stewed steak when arranged with balance has a pleasing brown background, but this is far too heavy; by adding julienne strips of carrot and turnip the dullness is relieved.

Blanc-mange when placed in a dish has a weak appeal to the eye; it is negative and somewhat insipid in colour. To correct this add cocoanut delicately tinted pink. The pink and white will harmonise and make a stronger appeal to the eye than would be the case if the blanc-mange was served without this garnish.

To colour various foods and garnishes such as blanc-mange, cocoanut, apples, icing sugar, the colours are produced as follows:

Red to Pink	Garmine or Cochineal.
Green to light Green	Apple-Green
Brown to light Brown	Chocolate Colouring.
Blue	Purvio Blue.
Yellow	Yellow Colouring.

The following methods of serving food are given as suggestions:—

Bacon.—Should be laid out in the dish like bread and butter on a plate.

Eggs Fried.—Laid on white dishes.

Sausages, Kidneys, Livers, Chops.—Pour brown gravy over them just before serving.

Haddocks.—Kept covered with very hot water, which should be strained off just before serving.

Tomatoes Fresh or Tinned.—Always serve in separate dishes, otherwise the tomatoes will sodden food, such as bacon, sausage or steak, etc.

Steaks and Onions.—Serve the steaks neatly arranged, the onions with a thick brown gravy, serve in separate dishes.

Haricot Beans (with bacon).—Are improved by mixing them with a very thin tomato sauce.

Boiled Fish.—Should be served with parsley sauce. If desired chopped parsley may be sprinkled lightly over the top.

Meats Roasted.—Neatly arranged, gravy poured over just before serving; where the joint is served whole, it may be garnished with vermicelli or sprigs of parsley.

Boiled Meats.—Serve with carrots and turnips cut into julienne strips, and placed in each corner of the dish just before serving.

Fruit Pies.—Dredge over with caster sugar.

Meat Pies.—Wash over with milk or weak solution of yolkene.

Cabbage.—Well strained, chopped and neatly pressed in white dishes.

Carrots and Parsnips.—Arrange in bundles.

Peas and Beans.—Arrange in white dishes with water over them, straining this off just before serving.

Cauliflower, Boiled Onions.—Serve occasionally with a white sauce.

Swedes, Turnips.—Should be mashed through a mincing machine, seasoned with pepper and salt and margarine, and arranged neatly in white dishes.

Canary, Patriotic and Sponge Puddings.—Serve in white dishes, jam sauce served around with coloured cocoanut sprinkled over the top.

Blanc-manges and Jellies.—Serve the blanc-manges from time to time in various colours; pink, light green, chocolate and tinted yellow. Jellies should be whisked or ribboned and cut into squares and served at the base of the blanc-manges.

Sultana and Currant Rolls.—Serve occasionally with white or pink sauce.

Milk Puddings.—Serve in white dishes, occasionally garnishing with chopped angelica.

CHAPTER II

COOKING IN SMALL QUANTITIES

Soups

THE STOCK-POT

As stock is the basis of most soups, sauces and gravies, it is important that the making of it should be thoroughly understood.

Sinewy, lean and gelatinous parts of meat, and a proportion of bone are suitable. Vegetables may be used such as carrots, onions and turnips, but should never be left in the stock after an infusion has taken place; neglect of this will lead to fermentation taking place and the stock being spoilt.

Whilst many scraps of cooked and uncooked meat, game and poultry trimmings may be used, yet there are certain things which must on no account be put in:—

(1) Food containing starch, such as bread, potato, rice, and sauces thickened with flour.
(2) Pork, salt or tainted meats.
(3) Fat.
(4) Cabbage in any form.

Proportions for making or starting a stock-pot.—2 lbs. of bones, 2 quarts of cold water, one small carrot, onion, turnip, salt.

1. Wash the bones, remove the fat, but not the marrow, saw into small pieces.

2. Put the bones in the stock-pot with the cold water and salt.

3. Bring slowly to the boil, keeping it well skimmed.

4. Wash, peel, and scrape the vegetables, add them and simmer for at least four hours.

5. If the vegetables are removed, the remainder can be left in the stock-pot. Draw off the stock as renewed.

GIBLET SOUP

Proportions.—4 sets of giblets, 1 carrot, onion, turnip, ¼ head of celery, 2 ozs. flour, 1 bay leaf, 2 cloves, 10 peppercorns, juice of half lemon, 2 quarts of stock, salt and pepper.

1. Wash the giblets, cut into small pieces, place in a saucepan with the stock, bring quickly to the boil and skim well.

2. Add herbs tied up in a muslin bag, bay leaf, celery, pepper and salt, simmer for 1½ hours.

3. Add the vegetables, simmer for another hour.

4. Strain, return to the saucepan, mix flour to a smooth paste with cold water, stir into the soup, boil for 5 minutes, add lemon juice.

5. Serve with some of the giblets trimmed into dice shape.

JULIENNE SOUP

Proportions.—2 quarts of good strong stock, 1 carrot, onion, turnip, 1 stick of celery, 1 bay leaf, pepper and salt to taste.

Cut the vegetables into fine shreds about an inch long, and boil in the stock until well cooked. Add seasoning.

MOCK TURTLE SOUP

Proportions.—½ tin calf's head, 2 ozs. ham, 1 carrot and 1 onion, 2 sticks of celery, ½ teaspoonful of parsley, ½ teaspoonful of thyme, 1 bay leaf, 1½ ozs. fat, 1½ ozs. flour, lemon juice, 5 pints boiling stock.

1. Melt the fat in a large stewpan, fry the ham and vegetables to a light brown colour, then sprinkle in the flour, let the ingredients cook slowly until well browned.

2. Drain the calf's head, add the liquor to the stock, cut the meat into neat pieces.

3. Pour the boiling water over the brown vegetables, add herbs in a muslin bag, boil up, skim well.

4. When the vegetables are tender, pass through a hair sieve.

5. Replace in a stewpan, bring to the boil and season, add lemon juice to taste, put the prepared meat and forcemeat balls into the hot soup. Serve thoroughly hot.

RICE CREAM SOUP

Proportions.—3 ozs. veal, 1 oz. rice, 1 pint milk, small onion, pepper and salt, stick of cinnamon.

1. Cut the meat into small pieces, wash the rice.

2. Put both in a saucepan with the milk, simmer very slowly for three hours.

3. Rub through a wire sieve and reheat, taking care not to boil.

4. It should be the consistency of rich cream.

SHEEP'S HEAD BROTH

Proportions.—1 sheep's head, 1 carrot, 1 turnip, 1 onion, 3ozs. barley, pepper, salt, 2 quarts of water, 1 bay leaf, ¼ teaspoonful celery seed, 2 peppercorns.

1. Clean the sheep's head, remove the brains and tongue. Soak in salted water for 12 hours, change the water about 3 times.

2. Place the sheep's head in a saucepan with a handful of salt, cover with cold water, bring to the boil, then strain.

3. Return to the saucepan, add 2 quarts water and bring to the boil, skim thoroughly, add teaspoonful salt, simmer 3 hours.

4. When the broth has been simmering 1½ hours, add vegetables, prepared in dice shape, herbs in a muslin bag, seasoning and barley.

5. Take out the head and herbs, remove the meat from the head, cut into dice shape.

6. Return the meat to the saucepan and reheat.

7. The brains can be utilised for brain cakes, the tongue cooked separately, and if desired only a small portion of the head need be served in the broth, the remainder could be served separately.

UNIVERSAL SOUP

Proportions.—2 quarts stock, 2 carrots, 2 onions, 2 turnips, 4 eschallots, bunch of sweet herbs, pepper and salt, stalk of cabbage.

1. Cut all the vegetables very fine, place in a saucepan with the stock, herbs, salt and pepper.

2. Simmer slowly for 2 hours, skim well.

VALETTA SOUP

Proportions.—3 ozs. vermicelli, 1½ pints stock, grated cheese, salt and pepper.

1. Bring stock to the boil, add pepper and salt.

2. Blanch the vermicelli in salted water, strain, place in the stock and cook about ½ hour, skimming well.

3. Just before serving add the grated cheese.

Fish

HOW TO DRESS A CRAB

1. Before boiling, kill the crab by piercing the eyes.

2. Place in a pot of boiling water with a handful of salt, and allow to boil twenty minutes or longer if required.

3. When cold, break off the large claws, then open the crab by separating with your hands the body from the top shell, in which there is a brown and white creamy matter.

4. Take this, and with salt, pepper and vinegar to taste, mix it with as much breadcrumbs as to get a solid paste.

5. Wash out the top shell, and fill each end with this paste, leaving a place in the middle for the white meat.

6. Before picking the white meat out of the body of the crab, clear away the fungus part (called the dead man).

7. Cut the white meat very small and fill in the shell between the brown paste.

8. Crack the claws, take out the meat, which, if carefully operated upon with a fork, will become finely shredded, and place this on top of the other white meat.

9. Take some finely chopped parsley and garnish around the bottom of the white part. Take the small claws or feelers, cut them at both ends, stick them together so as to form a chain, and lay round the dish on which the crab is served. Garnish dish with beetroot cut in shapes.

KEDGEREE

Proportions.—½ lb. boiled fish, ¼ lb. rice, 2 ozs. butter, ½ pint milk, 2 eggs, cayenne pepper, nutmeg, salt.

1. Blanch the rice in water and boil for ten minutes.

2. Strain off the water, and boil in half a pint of milk; the rice must be quite soft.

3. Boil the egg very hard, break the fish in pieces and carefully remove all the bones; cut the whites of the fish into small square pieces.

4. Melt the butter in a stewpan, add rice, fish, white of egg, cayenne pepper, a little grated nutmeg and salt. Mix them well together and serve on a hot dish, and sprinkle the yolks of eggs over it.

Dried haddocks make very nice kedgeree.

SOUSED MACKEREL

Proportions.—6 fresh mackerel, 12 peppercorns, 1 blade of mace, 1 gill of vinegar, ½ gill of water, salt.

1. Wash and clean the mackerel, cut off the heads and fins, remove the backbone carefully.

2. Roll up the fish and place them in a pie-dish.

3. Mix all the other ingredients together and pour over the fish.

4. Cover the dish closely with greased paper and bake in a moderate oven for about half an hour, serve cold.

Meat Dishes and Savouries

BAKED HEART

Proportions.—A calf's heart, 2 ozs. dripping, breadcrumbs, chopped suet, chopped parsley, thyme, marjoram, 1 egg or a little milk, salt and pepper.

1. Soak the heart in slightly warm water for an hour.

2. Mix together the breadcrumbs, chopped suet, parsley, herbs, salt and pepper, and bind these ingredients together with 1 egg or a little milk.

3. Dry the heart and trim the gristle parts away.

4. Stuff the heart with the stuffing.

5. Flour it, and place in a baking tin, pour a little cool fat over and bake in a steady oven.

HARICOT MUTTON

Proportions.—2 lbs. of scrag end or neck of mutton, 2 onions,

2 carrots and 2 turnips, 1 oz. dripping, 1 oz. flour, ¾ pint of cold water, salt and pepper.

1. Cut the mutton into pieces and fry it brown on both sides in the dripping.

2. Take out the meat and stir in the flour, allowing it to brown in the dripping.

3. Stir in three-quarters of a pint of water or stock, and put back the meat.

4. Cut the carrots, onions, and turnips into dice-shaped pieces, add these vegetables to the saucepan, season and skim well.

5. Simmer gently for two hours.

6. Serve meat in a circle, gravy over the top, vegetables in the centre.

POOR MAN'S GOOSE

Proportions.—½ lb. potatoes, ½ lb. pig's fry or scraps of pork or liver, 2 onions, dried sage, salt and pepper, 1 tablespoonful flour.

1. Mix the flour and seasoning together, cut the meat into pieces, dip each piece into the seasoned flour.

2. Lay these in a pie-dish alternately with the onion sliced thinly.

3. Parboil the potatoes, slice them and place over the meat, put the rest of the seasoning over the top, half fill the dish with cold water.

4. Cover with greased paper and bake for an hour.

STEWED RABBIT

Proportions.—1 rabbit, 3 oz. bacon, ¼ pint of milk, 2 onions, 1 tablespoonful of flour, 2 cloves, salt and pepper.

1. Cut the rabbit into pieces, let it soak in salted water for an hour.

2. Take out the rabbit, place in a saucepan with onions, cloves, bacon (cut into small pieces), add sufficient cold water to cover.

3. Simmer for one and a half hours.

4. Mix the flour, salt and pepper with the milk, add carefully to the rabbit and boil for five minutes.

Savouries

ANGELS ON HORSEBACK

Proportions.—6 oysters, 6 round croutons, 6 pieces of very thin bacon (2 inches long, 1½ inches wide).

1. Beard and trim each oyster, put one on each piece of bacon, sprinkle over the oyster a little cayenne, two drops of lemon juice.

2. Then roll it up in the bacon.

3. Lay each roll of bacon and oyster on a crouton, put them into a brisk oven to cook the bacon.

4. Serve very hot, dished up on watercress.

WELSH RAREBIT

Proportions.— ½ lb. cheese (grated or cut into small pieces), 1 oz. butter, 2 tablespoonfuls of milk, 1 teaspoonful of made mustard, hot buttered toast.

1. Melt the butter in a stewpan, add the cheese, stir until melted, then add the milk gradually, mustard and other seasoning to taste.

2. Have ready some buttered toast, pour the cheese preparation on to it, and serve as hot as possible.

Vegetables

The vegetables in common use in H.M. Service are potatoes, carrots, turnips, onions, cabbages, greens, turnip tops, beans, vegetable marrow, dried peas and haricot beans.

CABBAGES

Cabbages, greens, turnip tops, and green vegetables generally, must be first well picked, washed, and left in salt and water, heads downward, for a short time to expel any insects that may be in them.

They should then be placed in boiling water, to which has been added a piece of soda of a size in proportion to the amount of greens to be cooked. The soda will assist in retention of the colour of the vegetable, but should too much be used, the effect will be bad colour, unpleasant odour and bitter taste. Be careful to add the soda to the water *before* immersing the greens.

Cabbage is made more digestible and nutritious if it is boiled in two waters.

Leave cauliflower and Brussels sprouts whole.

CARROTS

Carrots should always be sent up to table with boiled beef. They vary much in quality, but should be quite firm, and have a crisp appearance when broken. Young carrots should be washed and well scrubbed before cooking; old ones will require scraping and cutting into quarters lengthwise. A little salt should always be boiled with them.

HARICOT BEANS (DRIED)

These should be thoroughly washed and then allowed to soak. Steep them overnight, throwing away the water and adding fresh for cooking purposes. Place them in a saucepan with four times their quantity of cold water. Let them come gradually to the boil and simmer gently from two to three hours until tender, stirring occasionally whilst cooking. The water they are boiled in makes excellent stock.

MARROWFAT PEAS (DRIED)

These are a valuable article of food, being highly nutritious, and when cooked properly are very palatable, resembling closely ordinary fresh green peas. Care must be exercised in the cooking. Excellent results have been obtained by the following method for large quantities:—

Soak the peas for 12 hours in a soda solution, allowing one pound of soda to every ten pounds of peas. Strain them, then wash well with plenty of cold water. Plunge into boiling water (without any soda), and cook gently for an hour. Add the salt just before they are cooked. If this routine is carried out, the peas will have a green colour similar to the fresh variety. After cooking they should be strained and washed with boiling water to remove all traces of soda.

ONIONS

On being boiled, an onion is deprived of much of its pungent, volatile oil, and becomes agreeable, mild and nutritious. As a slight flavouring, it is considered an improvement to all made dishes.

POTATOES

Potatoes are best when cooked in their skins, but when it is necessary to peel them, it should be done as thinly as possible, as the best part of the potato is that nearest the skin. After peeling, they should be kept in cold water until required for use.

When potatoes are very old, they acquire an unpleasant taste when boiled in their skins.

Sweets

COLLEGE PUDDING

Proportions.—6 ozs. flour, 4 ozs. currants, 2 ozs. breadcrumbs, 4 ozs. sugar, 4 ozs. suet, 2 eggs, milk.

1. Mix all the dry ingredients thoroughly.
2. Moisten with beaten eggs and a little milk.
3. Three parts fill some buttered moulds with the mixture,

cover with greased paper and steam for one and half hours. Serve with a sweet sauce.

PATRIOTIC PUDDING

Proportions.—4 ozs. flour, 2 ozs. butter, 2 ozs. caster sugar, 1 egg, ¼ pint of milk, 1 teaspoonful of baking powder, 3 tablespoonfuls of golden syrup, pinch of salt.

1. Sift the flour, baking powder and salt through a sieve into a basin.
2. Rub in the butter, add the sugar.
3. Beat up the egg, add the milk.
4. Stir these to the dry ingredients.
5. Butter a pudding basin, pour in the golden syrup, coat the basin with it, and put in the pudding mixture.
6. Cover with greased paper and steam for two hours. Turn out and serve.

SANDHURST PUDDING

Proportions.—2 eggs and their weight in butter and flour, 1 teaspoonful of baking powder, 3 tablespoonfuls of marmalade, 1 oz. caster sugar, 1 tablespoonful of milk, lemon sauce.

1. Sift the flour and baking powder on a piece of paper.
2. Cream the butter and sugar and beat the eggs one at a time, add marmalade, then the flour and milk.
3. Put the mixture in a greased basin, cover with greased paper and steam for one and half hours.

SWEET OMELET

Proportions.—3 eggs, 1 oz. sugar, 2 ozs. jam, ½ oz. butter.

1. Separate the whites from the yolks of the eggs, being careful to have a dry basin.

2. Beat up the whites to a stiff froth, after adding a pinch of salt.

3. Melt the butter in an omelet pan.

4. Fold the yolks into the whites lightly.

5. Put the mixture into the centre of the pan and place in a hot oven.

6. Warm the jam, turn out the omelet when done on to caster sugar.

7. Spread the jam over one half, then lightly draw a knife down the centre and fold over.

8. Place on a hot dish, sprinkle with caster sugar and serve hot.

TAPIOCA PUDDING

Proportions.—1½ ozs. tapioca, 1 oz. sugar, 1 pint milk, nutmeg, butter.

1. Soak the tapioca for half an hour.

2. Grease a pie-dish.

3. Place in the tapioca, sugar, milk and place the butter over the top in small pieces, and the nutmeg grated.

4. Set the pie-dish in a deep tin half filled with hot water, and bake in a moderate oven for three-quarters of an hour.

Sauces

A sauce supplies richness and flavour to foods which without their aid would be somewhat insipid, as for example caper sauce with boiled mutton and parsley sauce with boiled cod; on the other hand a sauce can counteract the richness of food, such as apple sauce with roast pork. Where acid is liable to predominate, as in fresh stewed fruits, a sauce has the power to modify the acid besides making the dish look appetising. The dryness of some boiled or steamed puddings is entirely overcome by the addition of a sauce, as, jam sauce with canary pudding.

Although there are many sauces, they are nearly all derived from a definite foundation. There are the standard *White* and *Brown* sauces from which a great variety of other sauces are made, and the chief garnish or flavouring of which creates the necessity for appropriate names.

HOW TO MAKE THE STANDARD WHITE SAUCE
Proportions for Coating Sauce.—1 oz. flour, 1 oz. butter, ½ pint of liquid.
Proportions for Flowing Sauce.—¾ oz. flour, ¾ oz. butter, ½ pint of liquid.

1. Melt the butter in a saucepan, draw aside.
2. Mix in flour smoothly with a wooden spoon, stir over gentle heat for 5 minutes, without allowing the mixture to brown. This is the first step in cooking the flour, heat and moisture causing capsules enclosing starch to rupture.

3. Draw pan aside again to cool, add liquid gradually, mixing it in with the flour and butter very smoothly.

4. Return pan to the fire, bring sauce to boiling-point stirring the whole time, cook for 7 minutes to ensure thorough cooking of flour. Season to taste.

HOW TO MAKE THE STANDARD BROWN SAUCE
Proportions the same as the White Standard Sauce.

1. Melt the butter in a saucepan, add the flour and cook until it is a deep rich brown colour.

2. Add the liquid very gradually, stirring the whole time for 7 minutes. The simmering and skimming of a brown sauce should be carried out very thoroughly as the flour in this type of sauce is liable to yield up some of the butter, and the grease will float upon the surface of the sauce.

GRAVY SAUCE
Pour the fat from a tin that has been used for baked meat, and add the quantity of stock necessary. Put the baking tin over the fire, season with pepper and salt, strain and remove the fat.

Pour around the joint or serve separately.

FESTIVE SAUCE
Proportions.—1 pint milk, 1 egg, 1 oz. sugar, ½ oz. cornflour, drops of vanilla essence.

1. Mix the cornflour with a little milk.

2. Boil the milk, then stand aside to cool a little, add sugar,

cornflour, stir until it thickens.

3. Beat the egg up in a basin, add to the sauce, just before serving add the vanilla essence. Vanilla essence, being a volatile oil, must be added at the very last, otherwise it will evaporate very quickly, with the result that the flavour will be lost.

CORRECT SAUCES TO SERVE WITH
MEAT AND POULTRY

Roast Beef	Horse-radish Sauce.
Grilled Steak	Tomato Sauce.
Roast Mutton	Onion Sauce.
	Red Currant Jelly.
Grilled or Fried Chop	Tomato Sauce.
Roast Pork	Apple Sauce.
	Brown Gravy.
Boiled Ham	Parsley Sauce.
Roast Lamb	Mint Sauce.
Roast Veal	Bread Sauce.
	Brown Gravy.
Calf's Head	Parsley Sauce.
Roast Chicken	Bread Sauce.
Roast Goose	Apple Sauce.
Roast Duck	Apple Sauce.
Roast Turkey	Bread Sauce.
Boiled Turkey	Celery Sauce.
Boiled Rabbit	Onion Sauce.
Roast Rabbit	Bread Sauce.
Jugged Hare	Brown Sauce.
	Red Currant Jelly.

Beverages, Small Quantities

TEA

Tea, if taken in moderation, is of dietetic value on account of its stimulating effects on the nervous system; on the other hand, if taken in excess, it will upset the digestive system and weaken the nerves.

Tea contains three active principles: Theine, Tannin and Volatile Oil.

The theine acts as a stimulating agent, the volatile oil gives off that characteristic aroma and fragrance peculiar to tea, and the tannin is an astringent. If the tea is infused too long, tannin is converted into tannic acid, and this is detrimental to the mucous lining of the stomach, interferes with digestion, and owing to the fact that it is an astringent, the drinking of tea should never follow the eating of meat. The binding power of the tannin hardens the already coagulated albumen of the meat, and this may lead to a state of constipation.

Tea should always be infused, that is the leaves should be steeped by pouring boiling water over them, but never allowing them to boil. If tea boils, it loses its fragrance because the volatile oil evaporates at boiling point.

"Cooked Water," that is water which has been boiling any time over two hours, should never be used for making tea. This water has lost its gases and is insipid. Freshly drawn water as soon as it has boiled one minute should be used, as it is then full of gases which will assist to extract the best flavour obtainable from tea.

COFFEE

Coffee has three principles: Caffeine, Tannin and Volatile Oil. The stimulation derived from coffee is due to the presence of the alkaloid called Caffeine; coffee is a stronger stimulant than tea, it stimulates not only the nerves but also the heart and makes the body more resistant to extreme cold. The characteristic aroma and fragrance of coffee comes from it volatile oil. The tannin in coffee is not so powerful as that obtained in tea.

In making coffee the cook should aim at extracting the pleasant flavours and aroma with their stimulating properties, avoiding the astringent or bitter ones.

Coffee, like tea, is made by infusion, so therefore should never be allowed to boil.

TO MAKE COFFEE FOR SMALL QUANTITIES

Proportions.—1 oz. coffee, 1 pint of boiling water.

1. Put the coffee on a tray and place in a warm oven for a few minutes.

2. Fill the coffee-pot up with boiling water, let stand for 5 minutes, then throw the water away.

3. Boil up some freshly drawn water.

4. Place the required amount of coffee in the pot, with a pinch of salt, add the boiling water, let it infuse for 5 minutes, add a little cold water, then strain.

5. Stand the strained coffee on the range for two minutes, serve up very hot with milk and sugar.

COCOA

Cocoa as a beverage is more nourishing than tea or coffee, but not so stimulating. It is more nourishing because it contains fat and starch. The Service cocoa contains all the cocoa fat, and arrowroot and refined sugar are added.

The slight stimulation derived from cocoa is due to the active principle of Theo-bromine. It also has an astringent similar to Tannin in action.

Cocoa is not made by infusion, and although it can be made in a similar manner, is really improved by boiling, because the starch thickens and makes it smoother in texture.

Navy chocolate is issued in block form and is described as soluble. The cocoa itself is not soluble in water, but is held in suspension by the starch contained in the arrowroot.

The best way to prepare Navy chocolate is to break it into small pieces and place in a saucepan, cover with sufficient water, and melt it down, stirring occasionally until it forms a thick paste.

TO MAKE COCOA FOR SMALL QUANTITIES

Proportions.—Cocoa ½ oz., water ½ pint, sugar ½ oz.

1. Place a teaspoonful of the cocoa paste (see above) into a pot, add half a pint of boiling water and simmer for half an hour.

2. Add milk and sugar, serve very hot.

CHAPTER III

COOKING FOR A GENERAL MESS

Introduction

The scales of ingredients given in the recipes in the following sections are intended to be a guide to the quantities required for the preparation of any particular meal. They are not intended to be a hard and fast rule, but should be adjusted when necessary by the Accountant Officer, who will be influenced by such factors as the following:—

Prices,

Shortage of supplies in any given commodity,

Season of the year,

Extraordinary service in which the ship is employed.

The quantities given are those of the various articles in a raw or unprepared state (e.g., weight of meat includes bone). The weight of the bulk of the meat without the bones should as a rule be taken after cooking and divided by the number victualled. This gives the ration of cooked meat per man. In preparing certain dishes the meat is weighed and distributed in mess tins, according to messes, before cooking, as indicated in the recipes.

The following systems are recommended for the distribution of the usual General Mess Meals:—

A NOTE ON TINNED FOOD

Salmon.—Should not be issued to the ship's company in tins. The cook, guided by the instructions as regards tinned food products, should open them, place in white dishes according to the numbers victualled in the messes.

Tinned Fruits.—Ascertain the number of pieces of fruit in each tin, decide the amount sufficient for one man. Usually a tin of fruit works out at one tin to eight men, the distribution can then be quickly made. Instead of counting all the fruit, if a mess has 26 men victualled for instance, then 3 tins can be opened and turned out into a dish and two men's rations counted in.

Breakfast Dishes

BACON AND KIDNEY OR LIVER

	100 Men.	500 Men.
Bacon	16 lbs.	80 lbs.
Liver	14 lbs.	70 lbs.

1. Cook the bacon in the usual manner.

2. Place a large fryer on the range with 2 inches of fat in it.

3. Cut the kidney or liver into suitable pieces, dry well, roll in seasoned flour, and when the fat has a blue vapour arising, place in the liver; cook to a golden brown.

4. Serve with thick brown gravy.

BOILED EGGS (2 PER MAN)

1. Half fill an iron tank with boiling water, place under a

steam-jet, continue to boil.

2. Place 500 eggs in the large strainer supplied to fit the tank and plunge into the boiling water for five minutes; then remove strainer from the tank and plunge the eggs into cold water. Unless this is done, the eggs on removal will continue to cook by their own heat until hard-boiled.

3. Remove the eggs from strainer and place in mess dishes according to galley distribution list, first placing in each dish sufficient cold water just to cover the bottom; put dishes in hot chests, where the eggs will remain hot and in good condition for eating for a quarter of an hour. When placing 1,000 eggs in the strainer to boil, allow eight minutes.

FISH CAKES

	100 Men.	500 Men.
Salmon	18 tins	90 tins.
Potatoes	31 lbs.	155 lbs.

1. Detail one section of the watch to prepare potatoes.

2. Detail one hand to inspect each tin of salmon. His observations must be strictly guided by the instructions on tinned food products contained at the beginning of Chapter VI.

3. Another section of the watch should open up the tins which have been passed by inspection, and strain off the liquor.

4. Whilst this is being done, cook the potatoes in a steamer, with a little salt sprinkled over them; when done,

pass through a mincing machine into a tank.

5. When the salmon has been turned out and strained, pass this through a mincing machine into a tank.

6. Pass salmon and potatoes together through a mincing machine the second time into a tank, so that the salmon and potatoes are thoroughly mixed together and now in one tank; add quarter of a pint bottle of anchovy essence to every 200 men, also pepper and salt to taste.

7. Weigh the whole and divide by the number victualled. This will give you the weight of each fish cake; approximately it will work out at three fish cakes to a pound.

8. Organise the watch as follows:—One rating weigh up the mixture at 1 lb. and make into rolls like a pound of butter, pass this roll on to the next rating, who will cut it into three, the next rating shape them up, egg-wash and breadcrumb; place into dishes.

9. Organise for frying by having ready three deep fryers on the range; one rating to do the frying. Place the fish cakes on baskets supplied to fit the fryers; when the oil is ready, plunge in the cakes, fry to a fine golden brown. In front of the range have a table covered with sacks, to put the baskets containing the cooked fish cakes on.

10. As each basket comes out of the fryer, unload quickly into dishes, and load up again with the raw cakes. Three fryers and three cooks can fry 1,000 fish cakes in an hour. When fish cakes are for breakfast, they should never be made overnight.

Dinners

MEAT DISHES

HARICOT MUTTON

	100 Men.	500 Men.
Mutton	43 lbs.	205 lbs.
Mixed Vegetables	12 lbs.	57 lbs.

1. Cut up the mutton into pieces about 2 inches long. Weigh the meat, and divide by the number victualled to arrive at the weight of meat for each man.

2. Weigh up the amount of meat for each mess, place in dishes and tally. Season with pepper and salt.

3. Prepare the vegetables, slice up, add to the meat, place dishes in a steamer, cook for one hour.

4. When done, strain off the liquor from the dishes into a tank, add some more stock, thicken up with flour mixed to a smooth flowing paste, season, add caramel colouring.

5. Pour a little of this rich, well-flavoured brown stock over the meat and vegetables in each dish (already tallied); place in the hot chests, ready for serving out.

BOILED CORNED PORK

	100 Men.	500 Men.
Pork	43 lbs.	205 lbs.

1. Place the joints of corned pork in dishes, place in the steamers, allowing 25 minutes to the pound for cooking.

2. Special attention must be paid to the amount of steam

pressure; about three turns of the steam valve should be sufficient.

SAUSAGES

	100 Men.	500 Men.
Sausages	25 lbs.	125 lbs.

1. Place 40 sausages in a mess dish, which has first been greased with half a pound of dripping or lard, and place in a hot oven to cook.

2. When cooked serve with thick brown gravy.

BATTER PUDDING

	100 Men.	500 Men.
Flour	12 lbs.	60 lbs.
Milk	4 tins	19 tins
Egg Powder	½ lb.	2 lbs.

1. Place the flour in a tank, season with salt, break the tinned milk down with cold water in bowls.

2. Mix milk and water into the flour; the consistency should be a creamy thickening.

3. Melt some fat in the service dishes.

4. Add egg powder to the mixture and mix well so as to beat as much air into it as possible, take out a bowlful at a time, sprinkle in a little baking powder, whisk quickly, pour a quart of the batter into a dish, bake in a very quick oven.

VEGETABLES

CAULIFLOWER

	100 Men.	500 Men.
Cauliflower	50 lbs.	238 lbs.

1. Trim the cauliflower, wash in salted water, cook separately the large outer leaves in a tank under the steam-jets, the same way as for cabbage.

2. Put the flower with a few inner leaves into white dishes, cover with greaseproof paper, and cook in a steamer until tender.

3. When distributing, serve an equal amount of flower and outer leaves to each mess.

BOILED TURNIP TOPS

	100 Men.	500 Men.
Turnip Tops	33 lbs.	157 lbs.

1. Trim the turnip tops, wash in salted water.

2. Place sufficient water in a tank under the steam-jets, bring to the boil, add soda.

3. Plunge in the turnip tops and, just before they are cooked, add salt, strain well, and place in dishes.

SWEETS

BANANAS DESSERT

One banana per man.

CANARY PUDDING

	100 Men.	500 Men.
Eggs	50 eggs	250 eggs
Margarine	6 lbs.	28 lbs.
White Sugar	6 lbs.	28 lbs.
Flour	6 lbs.	28 lbs.
Milk	4 tins	19 tins

Baking Powder, ⅛th oz. to every 4 ozs. of flour.

1. Cream the margarine and sugar together.

2. Break the eggs into it.

3. Add the milk, flour by degrees, beat in plenty of air, adding the baking powder lastly.

4. Place in greased basins, steam for two hours.

DOUGHBOYS

	100 Men.	500 Men.
Flour	6 lbs.	28 lbs.
Suet	1½ lbs.	7½ lbs.

1. Place the flour into a tank, add salt and baking powder (½ lb. to every 50 lbs. of flour), fold in the suet, mix with cold water to a plastic dough.

2. Cut into 2 oz. pieces, roll into balls, place in dishes covered with greaseproof paper, and steam for three-quarters of an hour.

ISLE OF WIGHT PUDDING

	100 Men.	500 Men.
Flour	6 lbs.	28 lbs.
Bread	3 lbs.	14 lbs.
Suet	1½ lbs.	7 lbs.
Syrup	3 lbs.	14 lbs.
Currants	3 lbs.	14 lbs.

1. Make a stiff paste with the flour, suet and water.

2. Prepare the breadcrumbs, warm the syrup, clean the currants, then mix these all together.

3. Roll the pastry to the size of a service dish, spread the breadcrumbs, syrup and currants over the pastry, wet the edges, roll up.

4. Place in greased dishes, steam two and a half hours.

QUEEN BESS PUDDING

	100 Men.	500 Men.
Flour	18 lbs.	86 lbs.
Suet	3 lbs.	14 lbs.
Sugar	3 lbs.	14 lbs.
Milk	2 tins	10 tins
Eggs	5 eggs	24 eggs
Cocoanut	6 lbs.	28 lbs.

1. Place the dry ingredients into a tank, mix the milk with water, stir in the eggs, then add to the dry ingredients, mix together.

2. Place everything into greased dishes or basins, and then

cook in a steamer (four hours for basins, two hours for dishes).

WINDSOR PUDDING

	100 Men.	500 Men.
Bread	6 lbs.	28 lbs.
Flour	3 lbs.	14 lbs.
Suet	2 lbs.	10 lbs.
Peel	12½ ozs.	4 lbs.
Currants	2 lbs.	10 lbs.
Raisins	2 lbs.	10 lbs.
Sugar	3 lbs.	14 lbs.
Potatoes	4 lbs.	19 lbs.
Carrots	3 lbs.	14 lbs.

1. Peel and shred the potatoes and carrots.
2. Clean the fruit, prepare the breadcrumbs.
3. Place all ingredients in a tank and mix to a plastic dough with cold water.
4. Place in greased dishes or basins and cook in the steamers (four hours for the service basins and two hours for the service dishes).

Teas and Cakes

TEAS FOR GENERAL MESSING

	100 Men.	500 Men.
Cake	31 lbs.	155 lbs.
Celery	25 heads	119 heads
Golden Syrup	12 lbs.	60 lbs.

Jam	12 lbs.	60 lbs.
Jellies	25 pints	125 pints
Lettuce	50 heads	238 heads
Margarine	3 lbs.	15 lbs.
Marmalade	12 lbs.	60 lbs.
Milk (fresh)	6 pints	30 pints
Milk (unsweetened)	2 tins	10 tins
Potted Meats	3 lbs.	15 lbs.
Radishes	72 bunches	360 bunches
Salmon	25 tins	125 tins
Sardines (4 oz. tin)	33 tins	165 tins
Shrimps	20 pints	100 pints
Sugar	4 lbs.	20 lbs.
Tea	1¼ lbs.	5 lbs.
Watercress	25 bundles	119 bundles

Suppers

BROWN STEW

	100 Men.	500 Men.
Beef	25 lbs.	119 lbs.
Tomatoes	10 tins	48 tins
Carrots	12 lbs.	57 lbs.
Turnips	6 lbs.	28 lbs.

1. Cut the meat up into fairly large pieces and cook in a steamer with the carrots and turnips.

2. When cooked, cut up the meat into dice-shaped pieces, pass the vegetables through a mincing machine.

3. Place the meat, vegetables, tomatoes, stock, caramel and

seasoning in a tank under the steam-jets, bring to the boil and thicken with flour.

4. Put into dishes and let the stew just simmer for half an hour in the ovens. Serve with mashed potatoes.

FAGGOTS AND PEAS

	100 Men.	500 Men.
Preserved Beef	12 lbs.	57 lbs.
Bacon	3 lbs.	14 lbs.
Liver	6 lbs.	29 lbs.
Bread	12 lbs.	57 lbs.
Onions	3 lbs.	14 lbs.
Herbs	1 packet	4 packets
Nutmeg	6 ozs.	1½ lbs.
Peas	6 lbs.	30 lbs.

1. Soak the bread for eight hours, then squeeze dry.

2. Cook the liver, bacon and onions, sprinkled over with herbs, pepper and salt, in a steamer.

3. Soak the peas for 12 hours in the following solution:— For every 10 lbs. of peas dissolve 1 lb. of soda in just sufficient water to cover the peas.

4. When the meat and onions are cooked, pass them through a mincing machine, with the preserved meat, into a tank; add the bread, nutmeg and season up, mix well together.

5. Put a tank under the steam-jets, add sufficient water but no soda, bring to the boil. Strain and wash the peas, then

plunge them into the boiling water and cook, adding salt just at the finish.

6. Weigh up the mixture, divide the weight by the number victualled to give the weight of a faggot per man (roughly three faggots to the pound). Place in dishes, put into the oven and brown the surface.

FISH AND CHIPS

	100 Men.	500 Men.
Fish	43 lbs.	185 lbs.
Potatoes	37 lbs.	176 lbs.

1. Clean the fish and cut to the required sizes. The potatoes may be peeled or well scrubbed.

2. Make a batter for frying the fish, add salt to taste.

3. Put the deep fryers containing the oil over a quick fire and bring to frying temperature.

4. Dip each piece of fish in the batter and fry 30 pieces at a time to a golden brown.

5. The potatoes should be chipped as required, salted, and fried a crisp golden brown.

6. To chip potatoes into water will cause them to lose their starch, take longer to cook, absorb the oil and become sodden, soft, pale and unpalatable.

Note:–A well-stoked, bright fire is necessary the whole time, and the orders referring to the depth of the oil in fryers should be strictly adhered to.

CHAPTER IV

SPICES, CONDIMENTS AND SEASONINGS

The most important articles used for seasoning and flavouring are salt, pepper, mustard, vinegar, sugar, cloves, allspice, cinnamon, nutmeg, ginger, aromatic herbs such as mint, sage, thyme, bay leaves, parsley, etc. They are mixed with various foods to render them more appetising and digestible, but only small quantities are used.

ALLSPICE

This spice is the berry of a plant which grows in the East Indies. It combines the flavour of cloves, cinnamon and nutmegs; hence the name. It is usually retailed in the powdered condition, and is also called Pimento or Jamaica pepper.

CLOVES

The clove tree belongs to the myrtle family. Cloves are the undeveloped flower buds. They are used to flavour soups, sauces and puddings, especially apple dishes, but care should be taken to use sparingly.

NUTMEGS AND MACE

Nutmegs and mace are both obtained from the fruit of the

nutmeg tree. The former are the kernels and the latter the fleshy, fibrous covering which surrounds them. The aromatic principles of the two spices are much alike, but mace contains nearly twice as much volatile oil as nutmegs. Both are used in various kinds of soups, jellies, puddings, spiced meat dishes, etc.

PEPPER

Black and white pepper are much adulterated with meal, etc., which tends principally to subdue the strength. It should have a pungent aromatic odour, and be hot and acrid to the taste.

CAYENNE PEPPER

Should be of a bright red colour. It has an aromatic, extremely pungent taste, and is very useful for flavouring purposes.

SALT

The finest is known by its whiteness, fine crystallisation character, dryness, and complete and clear solution in water. It improves the taste of food and prevents decomposition.

SUGAR

The sugar used in the Service is cane, known as Demerara, a crystallised yellow sugar of the finest quality and colour. Sugar, like salt, is both a preservative and a valuable food as

well as a useful flavouring ingredient. What salt is to meat
and vegetables, sugar is to all fruits and many farinaceous
foods, rendering palatable what would otherwise be insipid
or sour.

VINEGAR

The vinegar used in the Navy is of the description known as
Malt Vinegar. It is brewed in much the same manner as ordinary beer, but without the addition of hops. The malt is
mashed, and the wort is fermented with yeast. It is then
allowed to flow over piles of birch twigs, or wood shavings,
which are coated with a fungus called the vinegar plant,
because it induces acetic fermentation. The vinegar will be
found much stronger and more bitter than that usually sold
commercially.

SEASONING HERBS

A faggot of herbs usually consists of two sprigs of parsley,
four of savory, six of thyme, and two small bay leaves tied
together; marjoram may be added. A cook should be very
careful in recognising the commonest of all herbs, parsley,
fools' parsley or lesser hemlock being sometimes mistaken
for it. The latter is of a poisonous nature, and may be
detected by bruising the leaves, when they will emit an
unpleasant smell, unlike parsley.

CHAPTER V

INVALID COOKERY

The following recipes are intended for sick persons. The seasonings and flavourings recommended may have to be reduced, or omitted, in the case of weak or impaired digestions.

BENGER'S FOOD

Proportions.—1 large tablespoonful of Benger's Food, ½ pint milk.

1. Put the food into a basin and mix smoothly with a little of the milk.

2. Put the rest of the milk on to boil and, when boiling, stir on to the food. Allow it to stand for half an hour to digest partially.

3. Put back into the saucepan and stir well till boiling.

N.B.—The food must be mixed carefully to avoid lumps.

SHEEP'S OR CALVES' BRAINS

1. Well wash the brains in salted water several times.

2. Remove the skin, then blanch them in stock or water for five minutes, cook, dry before using. This preliminary preparation is always necessary.

3. Divide the prepared brains into neat pieces, dip into

seasoned flour, egg-wash and breadcrumb each piece carefully.

4. Fry in hot fat, garnish with fried parsley.

INVALID CHOP

Proportions.—1 mutton chop, 2 tablespoonfuls of water or stock, ½ oz. breadcrumbs and seasoning.

1. Shred the meat and put it in a pan with the other ingredients and seasoning.

2. Simmer for 10 minutes and serve on toast.

SAGO PUDDING

Proportions.—1½ ozs. of sago, 1 pint of milk, 1 oz. of sugar, 1 egg, nutmeg or flavouring.

1. Beat up the egg in a basin and add the sugar.

2. Put the milk in a saucepan with a little lemon rind and bring to the boil. Sprinkle in the sago, stir and boil slowly till sago is clear and transparent. Stir in the beaten egg.

EGG JELLY

Proportions.—2 lemons, 2 eggs, 6 ozs. sugar, 1 oz. gelatine, 1 pint of cold water.

1. Wash the lemons and peel very thinly, squeeze out the juice, make up to a pint with cold water and add this to the eggs beaten up.

2. Put all ingredients into a saucepan over a slow fire until the sugar and gelatine are dissolved, and the jelly begins to

thicken, but do not boil.

3. Strain and put into a mould to set.

JUNKET

1. To every quart of milk, sweetened and flavoured as desired, and warmed to 98° Fahr. (lukewarm), add a teaspoonful of rennet and stir once or twice only. If a junket tablet is used, dissolve it in half a teaspoonful of lukewarm water and add to the milk.

2. Leave in a cool place till set.

3. A little nutmeg may then be grated over it.

NOTE.—The heat of the milk must not be raised above 98° Fahr. Watered milk will not set properly.

Liquids

ALBUMEN WATER

Proportions.—Whites of 4 eggs, juice of half a lemon, 1 pint of cold water, 1 teaspoonful of sugar.

1. Beat up the whites of eggs, place in a jar or basin.

2. Add the cold water, lemon juice and sugar, let it stand until dissolved, when it is ready for use.

NOTE.—Use cold water, as white of egg coagulates at a temperature of 180° Fahr., and is then insoluble.

RAW BEEF JUICE

Proportions.—½ lb. beef steak, ½ pint water, ½-saltspoonful of salt.

1. Free the meat of fat and skin.

2. Scrape it finely, soak in cold water and salt for one to two hours. It must be stirred occasionally, and when strained the meat should be well pressed.

3. Raw beef tea does not keep well. It is most valuable in cases of extreme exhaustion and can often be taken when the stomach will retain nothing else.

NOTES ON BEEF TEA

Beef tea must never boil, and for this reason it is better made in a jar placed in a pan of water. Boiling makes the albumen hard, and prevents the extraction of the red juices. Preliminary soaking in cold water is most important, as this draws out the soluble nutritious properties. Rump or steak is far better than shin of beef for making beef tea.

BEEF TEA

Proportions.— ½ lb. gravy beef, ½ pint of water.

1. Cut the beef up very finely, removing all skin and fat.

2. Place into a stone jar with half a pint of cold water. Put the lid on the jar and cover with a piece of paper tied down.

3 Stand the jar in a saucepan of boiling water for 3 hours, or in the oven for 1½ hours; after that time strain the beef tea into a cup. Salt according to taste.

GRUEL

Proportions.—1 tablespoonful fine oatmeal, 1 pint of water, sugar, nutmeg (optional).

1. Take the oatmeal with a little salt and add by degrees enough cold water to mix it.

2. Add one teaspoonful of sugar and a little nutmeg.

3. Boil one pint of water.

4. When boiling, stir into the oatmeal, boil for 10 minutes.

5. If the oatmeal is course it must boil longer, and would be better strained before serving. Gruel, if properly made, should be as smooth as cream.

LINSEED TEA

Proportions.—1 oz. linseed, 1 quart of water, ½ oz. of liquorice, ½ oz. of sugar candy, strip of lemon rind.

1. Wash the linseed, place in a saucepan, with the cold water, add lemon rind.

2. Boil gently for one hour.

3. Add liquorice and sugar candy.

4. Strain and serve.

CHAPTER VI

MISCELLANEOUS

Precautions as regards Tinned Foods

When food products in tins are being used the tins should be first carefully examined for punctures, rust or signs of bulging at either end. Should a puncture or bulge be noticed, or the tin be rusted at the joints, it should not be opened, as the contents will almost certainly be bad. It should be returned into store with a report of the reason for doing so.

Tins should never be opened until the contents are actually required for cooking purposes, and the contents should be immediately transferred to earthenware or enamelled receptacles. When a number of tins are used, the contents of each tin should be carefully examined before being placed with the bulk.

Dishes containing tinned food as one of the ingredients, more especially when used in conjunction with potatoes, should be cooked as soon as made. Better to have to re-heat the dish before serving than to delay cooking.

The above directions are very important. Neglect of them will sooner or later result in trouble, and serious illness of the person or persons eating the food may easily be one of the consequences.

Tinned milk.—Each tin should be well shaken before opening in order to mix the contents completely, as the cream may have separated, or some lumpiness may have developed.

Milk is not necessarily bad if it is merely thick and lumpy; this may be due to over-concentration in manufacture. Try whipping up with warm water, when the lumps will probably break down and give a uniform solution.

The milk is unfit if it is: blown; sour; coagulated (giving a "curdy" solution in warm water); putrefying.

Avoid rough handling of cases of milk, as this may cause the seams of the tins to develop minute leaks, when decomposition will result.

Ship-made Articles

PORK BRAWN

	100 Men.	500 Men.
Pig's head	20 lbs.	100 lbs.
Bacon	1¼ lbs.	6 lbs.
Beef	4 lbs.	20 lbs.
Pimento	⅝ oz	3 ozs.
Gelatine	2 sheets	10 sheets
Cloves	13 cloves	65 cloves
Onions	3 onions	15 onions
Water	4 quarts	20 quarts

1. Clean pig's heads, removing eyes, brains and blood, soak in salt water for 24 hours.

2. Place in cold water, bring to the boil, allow to cook for two hours, skimming off any fat at intervals.

3. Allow to cook, cut the meat into dice shape, not too large, remove all rind and gristle such as the ears, etc.

4. Cut up beef and bacon, uncooked, into dice shapes also, and place all the meat into the liquor.

5. Tie pimento, cloves and onions in a muslin bag, add to the liquor, simmer for another hour, skim well, remove the muslin bag, dissolve the gelatine in water, then add.

6. Season with pepper and salt, allow to cook a little, then pour into wetted basins, filling them to the top. Allow to set.

NOTE.—Pig's head can be substituted by beef, mutton, or any other combination of meats.

Pickling Meat
TO SALT BEEF IN A BRINE TUB

To salt 300 lbs. of meat, dissolve 80 lbs. of coarse salt and 1lb. saltpetre in sufficient water to cover the meat. Test the brine with a raw potato; if it sinks, add salt until it rises again. Pickle for five days. In very hot weather the pickle must be watched closely, otherwise it ferments and turns sour. The most suitable joints for pickling are brisket, silverside and buttock steak.

Meat, Fish, Vegetables and Fruits in Season
JANUARY

Meats.—Mutton, beef, pork, rabbits.

Fish.—Haddock, whiting, bloaters, sprats, kippers, plaice, herrings, shrimps, cod.

Vegetables.—Cabbage, broccoli, sprouts, savoys, celery, parsnips, turnips, carrots, onions, potatoes, beetroot, swedes.

Fruits.—Apples, oranges, bananas.

FEBRUARY

Meats.—Mutton, beef, pork, veal, rabbit.

Fish.—Haddock, cod, bloaters, sprats, plaice, kippers, whiting, shrimps.

Vegetables.—Cabbage, broccoli, sprouts, savoys, celery, parsnips, turnips, carrots, onions, potatoes, beetroot, swedes.

Fruits.—Apples, oranges, bananas.

MARCH

Meats.—Mutton, beef, pork, veal, lamb, rabbit.

Fish.—Bloaters, cod, whiting, sprats, shrimps, kippers, plaice.

Vegetables.—Cabbage, broccoli, turnips, onions, potatoes, parsnips, savoys, beetroot, carrots, tomatoes, celery, swedes.

Fruits.—Apples, oranges, bananas.

APRIL

Meats.—Mutton, beef, pork, veal, lamb.

Fish.—Bloaters, shrimps, kippers, plaice, mackerel, whiting.

Vegetables.—Turnip tops, cabbage, onions, potatoes, beetroot, cauliflower, tomatoes, carrots, parsnips, turnips, swedes, broccoli.

Fruits.—Oranges, rhubarb, apples, bananas.

MAY

Meat.—Beef, mutton, lamb, veal.

Fish.—Herrings, shrimps, plaice, whiting, mackerel, kippers.

Vegetables.—Early cabbage, new potatoes, turnips, swedes, carrots (new), cauliflower, lettuce, onions, radishes, cress, cucumbers, broccoli, tomatoes, beetroot.

Fruits.—Apples, rhubarb, oranges, bananas.

JUNE

Meats.—Beef, mutton, veal, lamb.

Fish.—Soles, whiting, mackerel, kippers, plaice, herrings, shrimps.

Vegetables.—Carrots, turnips, broccoli, potatoes, peas, cauliflower, onions, lettuce, cabbage, tomatoes, beetroot, swedes.

Fruits.—Apples, cherries, rhubarb, bananas.

JULY

Meats.—Mutton, beef, veal, lamb.

Fish.—Herrings, whiting, soles, plaice, kippers, mackerel, shrimps.

Vegetables.—Carrots, turnips, new potatoes, peas, onions,

cabbage, lettuce, beetroot, beans (broad and runner), cauliflower, vegetable marrows, broccoli, tomatoes, swedes.

Fruits.—Cherries, gooseberries, black and red currants, strawberries, apples, bananas.

AUGUST

Meats.—Mutton, beef, veal, lamb.

Fish.—Kippers, plaice, shrimps, herrings, whiting, haddock, hake.

Vegetables.—Carrots, turnips, new potatoes, peas, beans (runner and broad), cauliflower, onions, cabbage, lettuce, tomatoes, beetroot, vegetable marrow, broccoli, swedes.

Fruits.—Apples, cherries, plums, damsons, black and red currants, greengages, gooseberries, bananas.

SEPTEMBER

Meats.—Mutton, beef, lamb, rabbits, pork, veal.

Fish.—Herring, bloaters, haddocks, whiting, plaice, shrimps, kippers.

Vegetables.—Potatoes, celery, cucumbers, peas, beans (runner and broad), cauliflower, lettuce, carrots, turnips, cabbage, broccoli, sprouts, vegetable marrow, onions, tomatoes, beetroot, swedes.

Fruits.—Blackberries, damsons, apples, plums, black and red currants, gooseberries, greengages.

OCTOBER

Meats.—Mutton, beef, pork, veal, rabbits.

Fish.—Bloaters, shrimps, whiting, haddock, herrings, plaice, kippers.

Vegetables.—Cauliflower, sprouts, onions, tomatoes, lettuce, cabbage, potatoes, beetroot, vegetable marrow, celery, carrots, turnips, swedes, broccoli.

Fruits. —Apples, oranges, bananas, damsons, plums.

NOVEMBER

Meats.—Mutton, pork, veal, beef, rabbits.

Fish.—Herrings, cod, shrimps, plaice, haddock, kippers, sprats, whiting, bloaters.

Vegetables.—Cauliflower, sprouts, tomatoes, savoys, parsnips, celery, carrots, turnips, swedes, broccoli, onions, potatoes, cabbage, beetroot.

Fruits.—Apples, oranges, bananas.

DECEMBER

Meats.—Mutton, beef, pork, rabbits.

Fish.—Bloaters, herrings, haddock, whiting, sprats, cod, plaice, kippers, shrimps.

Vegetables.—Sprouts, savoys, celery, carrots, parsnips, turnips, onions, broccoli, cabbage, beetroot, potatoes, swedes.

Fruits.—Apples, oranges, bananas.

Miscellaneous Hints

THE FLY DANGER

The fly is one of man's greatest enemies and carries the germs of disease to any uncovered food, liquid or solid.

Breeding Places.—Refuse, litter, manure heaps, fermenting food stuff, fresh and decaying carcases, rotting vegetation, etc. Maggots cannot breed in dry refuse.

Preventive Measures.—Food cooked or uncooked, liquid or solid, should be kept always covered. Flies should be killed at every opportunity.

TANGLEFOOT

Heat together castor oil, five parts by weight, and powdered resin, 8 parts by weight, until the resin is completely dissolved. The mixture should not be brought to the boil. Apply whilst warm (or warm it before application), and, as thinly as possible, spread on glazed strips of paper (because unglazed paper absorbs the oil, thus destroying the adhesive properties of the mixture), or on narrow picture wire, to be hung vertically.

NOTE.—During the day, flies prefer broad surfaces, such as the paper, and the hanging wires by night.

SOAP

Put the issue of soap, soft soap and soda which is drawn from the Central Stores into a large pot. Add in weight the same amount of old fat, skimmed from the stock tank, also a little water. Simmer for two hours. Allow to cook, and it will form into a large cake of white soap. When required, put a little of this mixture into a bowl, pour boiling water on it and whisk briskly. A fine soapy mixture for any purpose in the galley will be the result.

POLISHING THE GALLEY

To produce a brilliant and lasting polish on a galley, mix vinegar with blacklead and clean in the usual manner, then paint over with varnish. Parts of the range which get very hot, such as the tops, cannot be treated in this manner.

EGG TESTER

This solution is a very good egg tester:—Mix 2 ozs. of salt with a pint of cold water in a service measure. The good eggs will sink in this solution, the bad ones will float.

MAKING LEMONADE

In making lemonade it is better to put the peel of the lemons in a jug, pour boiling sweetened water on it, and to add the juice of the lemons when the liquid is cold.

Home-made lemonade is sometimes bitter because some of the white pith is left on the lemon rind; care should be taken to peel the lemons very thinly.

SANDWICHES

Sandwiches will keep fresh for a long time if covered with

fresh lettuce or cabbage leaves and a damp cloth. It is an advantage if they can be kept in a tin box.

HOT GREASE

If hot grease be spilled on the table, pour cold water on it at once. This will cool the grease, which can then be scraped off, instead of its being allowed to sink into the wood.

TINWARE

If new tinware is rubbed over with fresh lard and thoroughly heated in the oven before it is used, it will never rust afterwards.

MEAT PUDDING

When lining a basin for meat pudding, cut a piece of the paste away from the bottom, about the size of a two-shilling piece. Then put the meat in as usual, and it will be found that the pudding will take an hour less to cook than if fully lined in the ordinary way.

CHAPTER VII

BREADMAKING

Bakery Routine

The following routine, for the guidance of bakers on board H.M. ships, is suggested as a convenient one to follow.

It may, however, be found necessary to alter the times, etc., in order to meet the requirements or fit in with the prevailing conditions of the bakery.

TIME	DUTY
On commissioning	The Chief Baker should examine his oven, dough mixer, and general bakery fittings, and report to the Accountant Officer as to their working condition.
	Draw hops and malt and proceed to brew yeast (2 pints of old yeast, or 2 ozs. of fresh compressed yeast would be required to start the brew). Time required, from 36 to 48 hours. Sponges to be set overnight at 8, 9, 10, and the fourth on turning out. The Chief Baker to use discretion regarding the temperatures at which they are set.
4.0 a.m.	Call Duty Hand and make fourth sponge, light fires.

4.45 a.m.	Make first dough.
5.30 a.m.	Cut back first dough.
6.0 a.m.	Chief Baker turn to. Make second dough.
6.15 a.m.	Scale off first dough.
When ready	Set first dough in oven. Cut back second dough.

Doughs to follow on at intervals of approximately two hours.

Routine for 10 lb. tins—approximate time for baking, 1½ hours per batch.

Chief Baker to arrange for cleaning up of bakery, scrubbing sponge and yeast tubs, etc., as convenient.

SUBSTANCES INJURIOUS TO YEAST

There are certain substances which have a deleterious effect upon the yeast cell; in small quantities they retard, in large quantities they altogether arrest the fermentation. Amongst others are lemon essence, mustard, carbolic acid, yokine, and salt in excess.

BREADMAKING IN THE TROPICS

In the tropics, or in very hot weather, it will sometimes be found an advantage to put a little salt (about 1 oz. to the gallon) into the wort at the time of starting fermentation. This will tend to steady the process of fermentation and prevent exhaustion and subsequent sourness.

BREAD DISEASES

Although every detail connected with breadmaking may be carried out correctly, there is still a danger of infection of the bread by micro-organisms which produce bread diseases.

One of these converts the bread to such a condition that it can be pulled into threads. The crumb becomes sticky, discoloured, and a disagreeable odour is noticed.

If in baking it is found that the crust does not assume a good brown colour although the correct baking temperatures have been maintained, the cause may be due to parasites in the flour commonly known as mites.

A simple test to find if mites are present, is as follows:—

Flatten the surface of a small quantity of flour by pressure with a knife or any other flat object, and leave it in that condition. If the flour contains mites the surface will soon become covered with small eruptions.

DANGER OF CARBON DIOXIDE POISONING

Care is to be taken that the bakery is kept well ventilated while the sponge is in the process of fermentation and while the dough is rising. During both these processes carbon dioxide gas is generated, and the escape of this gas when the sponge works or when the dough is over-ripe may be prejudicial to the health and even dangerous to the life of men remaining in a small, confined space without ventilation.

In no circumstances is any man to be permitted to sleep in the Bakery.

DOUGH MIXING AND KNEADING MACHINES.

The Senior Cook Rating in charge of the Bakery should especially impress upon the junior ratings the danger of tampering with the safety locking device fitted to these machines and of attempting to handle the dough while the knives are in motion.

Hurt Certificates will not be granted in case of accidents due to neglect or disobedience of this order and a notice to this effect is to be prominently displayed in all bakeries.

When the slippery condition of the deck in the bakery renders it advisable, steps are to be taken to fit cocoanut matting for battening down on the deck.

Further Reading

Henry Baynham, *Men from the Dreadnoughts* (London: Hutchinson, 1976), Chapter 9

D.K. Brown, *Nelson to Vanguard: Warship Development 1923–1945* (London: Chatham, 2000)

D.K. Brown and G. Moore *Rebuilding the Royal Navy: Warship Design since 1945* (London: Chatham, 2003)

Christopher McKee, *Sober Men and True – Sailor Lives in the Royal Navy 1900–1945* (Cambridge, Massachusetts: Harvard University Press, 2002), Chapter 3

A Note on the Text

The material reproduced in the preceding pages is a selection from the Admiralty's 1930 *B.R.5 Manual of Naval Cookery*, and it follows the sequence of the original publication. A few, minor stylistic changes were made to aid the modern reader.

Mark Hawkins-Dady was the editor of *Brinestain and Biscuit*, and Rosie Anderson converted the text to electronic form. Ken Wilson produced a fine design for it, and Fintan Power proofread most efficiently. Last but not least, Catherine De Gatacre brought this intriguing publication to the Archives' attention in the first place, so in a very real sense enabled this edition to emerge: many thanks to her.